Abraham Lincoln

ROAD TO
THE WHITE HOUSE

Abraham Lincoln

ROAD TO
THE WHITE HOUSE

By Keith Brandt and JoAnn Early Macken
Illustrated by John Lawn

SCHOLASTIC INC.
New York   Toronto   London   Auckland   Sydney
Mexico City   New Delhi   Hong Kong   Buenos Aires

ISBN-13: 978-0-439-88005-3
ISBN-10: 0-439-88005-X

12 11 10 9 8 7 6 5 4 3 2 1   7 8 9 10 11 12/0

Printed in the U.S.A.
First printing, January 2007

CONTENTS

CHAPTER 1:

Brand-New Babe

The sun pushed its way over the horizon. Its golden light chased away the shadows of the woods around the cabin near Hodgenville, Kentucky. The air stayed chilly on the morning of February 12, 1809.

Inside the one-room log cabin, it was nearly as cold. But the people in the room were too busy and excited to care about that. Tom Lincoln sat on a chair in one corner, talking to Sarah, his two-year-old daughter.

"Your mother will be just fine," he said. "You sit right here on pappy's lap and don't worry about a thing."

A few moments later, they heard the loud wail of a baby. The infant, named Abraham after his grandfather, had a strong voice. He was a large baby, sturdy and healthy looking.

Elizabeth Sparrow, little Abraham's great-aunt, had come to the cabin to help out. Elizabeth and her husband Tom Sparrow were foster parents to both Nancy Hanks Lincoln—Abraham's mother—and Dennis Hanks, Nancy's nine-year-old cousin.

Dennis would always remember the
day he first saw Abraham Lincoln. When
Dennis entered the cabin, he saw Nancy
Lincoln lying in bed, looking tired,
but happy. Tom Lincoln had thrown a
bearskin over Nancy and built a great
fire to keep her warm.

Elizabeth, sometimes called Betsy,
washed and dressed the new baby. Dennis
asked if he could hold little Abe. Nancy

said, "Yes, but be careful." She handed him the squirming infant.

Dennis thought the baby was homely. As soon as Abe was in his cousin's arms, he began to wail. The more Dennis tried to soothe him, the louder Abe cried. At last, Dennis handed the baby back to Betsy. "Take him!" Dennis said. "He'll never come to much."

CHAPTER 2:
Early Memories

Sinking Spring Farm was Abe's home for the first two years of his life. Then Tom Lincoln got tired of trying to grow crops in poor, rocky soil. He moved his family to a farm at Knob Creek, about ten miles away. As soon as they got there, Mr. Lincoln, a skilled carpenter, set to work building a log cabin and furniture.

It was easier for Tom Lincoln to make new furniture than to carry old furniture from one place to another. When the family settled in a new place, they had to

cut down many trees to clear the land for
farming. They used the wood to build a
cabin, furniture, and fences. They still had
plenty left over for firewood.

Like most pioneer children, Abe and Sarah helped with the chores. When he was big enough, Abe cleaned ashes from the fireplace. He filled the wood box with dry branches he collected in the forest. He hauled water from the creek. And he did anything else his parents asked him to do. Sarah helped her mother tend to the farm animals, do the cooking and baking, wash the clothes, and tidy the cabin.

Abe's earliest memories of childhood were of those days at Knob Creek. "I remember very well," he wrote, "our farm was composed of three fields which lay in the valley surrounded by high hills and deep gorges. . . . One Saturday afternoon, the other boys planted the corn in what we called the Big Field—it contained seven acres and I dropped the pumpkin seed. I dropped two seeds every other hill and every other row. The next Sunday morning there came a big rain in the hills; it did not rain a drop in the valley, but the water coming down through the gorges washed ground, corn, pumpkin seeds, and all clear off the field."

Life was a struggle for frontier families like the Lincolns. They needed every bit of food they could grow to feed themselves through the year. One long dry spell or bad flood could destroy a

whole year's crops. Such a loss brought terrible hardship to the farm families. They barely stayed alive, eating berries and nuts from the forest and any game they could hunt. Living this way was tough enough in warm weather, but it could mean starving in the winter.

CHAPTER 3:
Work and Play

Life wasn't all work for young Abe. He spent lots of time exploring the woods, fishing in the creek, and hunting with his father and the dogs.

A boy growing up in Kentucky could find many exciting things to do—and dangerous things, too. One day, Abe was out playing with his friend, Austin Gollaher. The boys wanted to cross Knob Creek. Rain had made the creek's waters deep and treacherous, but that didn't stop the boys.

The only way across the creek was to walk over a log that stretched from one side to the other. Abe went first, and he fell in halfway across. Neither boy could swim! Austin held out a long pole to Abe, who grabbed it, while Austin pulled him to shore.

Nancy Lincoln knew there were many dangers in the forest, and she was strict with her son when she had to be. But most of the time, she was sweet, gentle, and loving. She wanted only the best for her children. So, when a school opened down the road, Abe and Sarah were enrolled.

Zachariah Riney's one-room schoolhouse was a two-mile walk from the Lincoln home. It was a log cabin with a dirt floor. The window holes were covered with greased paper to let in a little light. Mr. Riney taught, "reading, writing, and ciphering." A student who did not behave felt the sting of a hickory stick.

The pupils learned their ABCs, how to spell a few words, and how to do simple arithmetic. The children said all their lessons out loud. This kind of school was called a "blab school" because it sounded so noisy.

The school was not free, but few frontier parents had money to pay for their children's schooling. Some paid the teacher with a bushel of corn or potatoes or a smoked ham. Others paid with skins from animals they had trapped, a cord of firewood, or anything else the teacher was willing to take.

The Lincoln family rarely used cash. They grew their own food. They made their own clothes out of animal hides or cotton or flax that they grew. They only wore shoes in the winter, and they made those, too. When they bought coffee or sugar from the store, they paid for it with meat or coonskins. If they worked for someone else, they were paid in goods, not money.

CHAPTER 4:
A Difficult Move

The Lincoln children did not attend Mr. Riney's school for long. In 1816, when Abe was seven, the Lincolns decided to move from Kentucky to Indiana. Abe's father chopped down trees, cut them into logs, and built a flatboat on Knob Creek. He and the boys loaded a chest full of tools and some of their furniture onboard. He sold the farm for ten barrels of whiskey plus twenty dollars. He loaded the barrels onto the boat, too.

Abe's father floated down the Salt
River to the Ohio River. Along the way,
the boat tipped. The tool chest and four
barrels of whiskey slid off. He was able
to find some of the missing things on
the bottom of the river. He crossed to
Indiana, claimed a plot of land, and left
the family's goods there. Then he walked
back to Kentucky to fetch his family.

In December of that year, with frost
covering the ground, the Lincolns left Knob
Creek forever. They traveled northwest
through forests, across the Ohio River, and
into Indiana. After a rough hundred-mile
journey, they reached their new home in
the wilderness at Little Pigeon Creek.

The first thing the Lincolns did was build a shelter. With snow falling steadily, the whole family worked to put up a simple shed. It had three walls made of logs and a roof of branches and bark. The south side, away from most of the wind and snow, was open. Their new land cost two dollars an acre.

At the open side, a blazing fire burned day and night. Nancy Lincoln cooked over the flames during the day. At night, the fire scared off wild animals. It also kept the family from freezing as they slept on piles of leaves under blankets and bearskins.

The shed was cozy as long as the weather was pleasant. In storms, rain and snow flew inside. If the wind blew from the south, smoke blew in with it, and the family had to leave their shelter.

Much of their furniture had been left

behind in Kentucky. Tom planned to make beds, tables, and chairs as soon as he had time to build a real cabin. But first, before beginning the cabin, he had to cut down some trees.

Abe worked beside his father. He trimmed branches from the trees his father cut. It took them weeks to chop down enough trees to build a cabin. There were so many other things to do every day—keep the fire at the camp blazing, fetch water from the spring a mile away, clear the land of stumps and stones to ready it for spring planting, and hunt for game to eat.

In the woods, the family found plenty of wild game—deer, bears, squirrels, raccoons, and rabbits. Years later, Abe remembered the day he shot his first— and only—wild turkey. When he saw he had hit the bird, he felt like a real hunter.

He was proud to bring food to the table. But when he saw the dead bird fall, he felt sad. From that day on, Abe did not like the idea of killing. This feeling stayed with him for the rest of his life.

CHAPTER 5:
Hard Times

The Lincolns' cabin was ready early that spring, and the family was glad to have a real home again. It was just one room, like their Knob Creek home had been. The bare dirt floor was packed and smoothed down. The chimney outside was plastered with clay, and a fire burned inside for light and heat. Animal skins hung over the window and door holes. Pegs in one wall formed a ladder that led to a loft over part of the cabin, where Abe slept on a bed of leaves. Rain and snow often

slipped inside through cracks in the roof.

In the fall of 1817, Tom and Betsy Sparrow and Dennis Hanks joined the Lincolns in Indiana. They moved into the three-sided shed. Both families suffered through the cold winter. They lived mostly on berries, nuts, and whatever wild game they could catch. Even so, the Lincolns were glad to have their relatives close.

Their happiness didn't last long. In the summer of 1818, Tom and Betsy Sparrow both fell ill with "milk sickness." It was caused by drinking milk from cows that had eaten poisonous plants. Nancy nursed her aunt and uncle, but no one knew of a cure for the illness. The Sparrows both died that fall. Not long after, Nancy became ill, too. She died of the same sickness. Dennis Hanks became part of the family, and he slept in the loft with Abe.

The world was a drab and lonely place

for the Lincoln family. Sarah did her best to cook and clean, but she was only twelve. Abe worked hard with his father and Dennis out in the fields. But the spirit had gone out of all of them. Their clothes grew ragged, and the house got dirtier and dirtier.

CHAPTER 6:
A Family Again

About a year after his wife died, Tom Lincoln took a trip back to Kentucky. He told the children to be good and take care of themselves until he came back. He rode off into the woods, promising to return as soon as he could.

It was a frightening time for the youngsters. At night, they heard bears and panthers in the woods. During the day, Dennis shot quail and rabbits for dinner. Abe and Sarah gathered nuts and berries in the woods. Abe ground corn for Sarah to bake into bread. Living this way wasn't easy, but it kept them from thinking too much about their fears and loneliness.

One day in December, the children heard something coming through the woods. They ran out of the house and saw their father leading a team of four horses harnessed to a covered wagon.

Tom helped a woman down from the wagon. She was tall and had a gentle smile. She was Sarah Bush Johnston, a woman Tom had known before he and Nancy were married. Sarah's husband had died, and Tom had gone back to Kentucky to ask her to marry him.

Sarah put her arms around the Lincoln children. "I'm mighty pleased to meet you," she said. "Now come and meet my children."

She led Abe, Sarah, and Dennis to the wagon. There, they met her two daughters, Elizabeth and Matilda, and her son John. Life at Little Pigeon Creek would be lonely no more. Abe and Sarah were part of a real family again.

CHAPTER 7:
A Fresh Start

The second Mrs. Lincoln made some much-needed changes. First, she had Abe, Dennis, and John fill a trough with water. She put out a gourd full of soap and one for dipping water. Then she told the boys to scrub themselves clean.

Tom's new wife had brought good furniture, pewter dishes, feather pillows and mattresses, pots and skillets, a flax wheel, and a soap kettle back from Kentucky with her. She left them all outside until the house was clean. She had

Tom put down a wooden floor and build
a real door and windows for the cabin.
She had the boys whitewash the walls and
ceiling. She emptied the old mattresses,
refilled them with fresh corn husks, and
put feather beds and clean bedding on top.

"Now," she said, "we have a proper
home!"

Abe liked his stepmother from the
start. She was a kind, intelligent woman
with a good sense of humor. She also
brought something Abe wanted—books.
Abe loved to read, and Sarah Lincoln
thought that was just fine.

Tom Lincoln would have liked Abe to forget about "book-learning" and get on with farming. Tom could read a little and sign his name, and he thought that was enough. His wife told him Abe was going to be a great man someday and should be educated. So, whenever the school near Little Pigeon Creek was open, she encouraged Abe to go. He did not spend much time in school, though. All together, his schooling added up to less than one year.

CHAPTER 8:
Always a Reader

Abe enjoyed school and did his work carefully and well. In one of his notebooks, between neat rows of numbers, he wrote:

Abraham Lincoln is my name
And with my pen I wrote the same.
I wrote in both haste and speed
and left it here for fools to read.

The tall, thin boy was always reading or thinking about reading. Before setting out to plow the fields in the morning, Abe would put a book inside his shirt and fill

his pockets with corn bread. When noon
came, he'd sit under a tree, reading and
eating at the same time. In the house at

night, he'd tilt a chair next to the chimney and read.

About his passion for reading, Abe said, "The things I want to know are in books; my best friend is someone who'll give me a book I haven't read."

There was no library in his part of the country. Most people did not own books. Abe tracked down the few books to be found nearby. He read the Bible, *Aesop's Fables*, *Robinson Crusoe*, *Pilgrim's Progress*, and a dictionary. Once, he walked twenty miles to borrow a book. Another time, a farmer lent him a biography of George Washington. After he finished reading, Abe tucked the book into a corner of the loft. While he slept, a storm came up. Rain poured through the roof and stained the book cover.

To pay for the ruined book, Abe spent two days harvesting corn for the farmer.

Even as a youngster, and even when it meant doing hard work, Abe was always truthful and ready to take responsibility for his deeds.

Two books meant a lot to him as a
teenager. One was full of facts about
geography, science, and world history
which encouraged his curiosity about

the world around him. The other was an Indiana law book. Abe read it over and over until he almost knew it by heart. He read about the Constitution and the Declaration of Independence. He wanted to learn everything he could about how laws worked and how they could be used for the good of people.

Years later, Abe became a lawyer, even though he didn't go to school for it. He did it by reading every law book he could get his hands on.

CHAPTER 9:

Growing, Growing, Grown

As Abe grew older, he kept growing
taller. His ankles always stuck out of
his pants. Because he had been working
most of his life, he was also strong. He
had cleared fields, plowed land, and split
logs to make fences. He learned carpentry
from his father. He worked for other
farmers, butchering livestock and digging
wells. At sixteen, he ran a ferryboat across
the Ohio River. He was already more than
six feet tall.

At eighteen, Abe built a flatboat and carried passengers and their belongings from shore out to steamboats in the river. In 1828, because of all his experience, he was hired to take a long river trip.

A local storekeeper wanted to sell a boatload of goods in New Orleans. Abe and the storekeeper's son took the boat more than a thousand miles down the Ohio and Mississippi Rivers. In New Orleans, they were amazed to see slaves for sale in markets. Abe never forgot the sight.

They sold the goods and the boat and took a steamboat back up the river. Abe earned eight dollars a month for the three-month trip. He gave all the money to his father.

After Abe got back home, his family moved again. Tom Lincoln had heard about the rich soil and open prairies in

Illinois. He sold his land and livestock, and the family settled near Decatur in the central part of the state. Once again, they cleared land, built a cabin, plowed the earth, and planted crops.

Abe split wood to build fences around their land. This work earned him the nickname "Rail Splitter," which stuck with him for the rest of his life.

That winter, a terrible blizzard hit the area. Deep snow piled up, and the temperature fell below zero. Horses and cattle froze to death. Bitter winds blew right through the rustic cabins. Both food and firewood were hard to find. No one wanted to stay there for another winter.

In 1831, Abe made another trip down the Mississippi River to New Orleans. A businessman hired him and two other men to carry a load of produce to sell. First, they spent about a month building the boat. They loaded it with corn, barrels of pork, and thirty live hogs.

While they built the boat, the water level in the river dropped. When they left, the boat stuck on a dam. The bow, or front end, pointed up in the air. Water poured into the stern, or back end. Abe drilled a hole in the bow. He rolled the barrels up to the bow to tip the boat forward, and the water ran out. Then he plugged the hole. The boat moved over the dam, and they continued their trip.

While Abe was gone, his family moved one more time. This time, they went southeast to Goose Nest Prairie, Illinois. At twenty-two, on his own at last, Abe became a clerk in a general store in New Salem, Illinois. He worked for the businessman who had sent him to New Orleans.

CHAPTER 10:

Speaking to the People

Abe was different from his friends and neighbors, but he was well liked. He was a great storyteller and had a wonderful sense of humor. That was important to people in those days.

Folks gathered at the store even when they had nothing to buy. They entertained themselves by swapping tales and gossip. Being a good storyteller was a matter of pride, and each person tried to outdo the others. Abe, who had been shy for a long time, "got the hang of talking," in front of

the story-swappers at the store. He soon became the best storyteller for miles around.

That young storyteller grew up to become one of the finest public speakers in American history. In New Salem, he joined a debating society and practiced speaking in public. As a member of the Illinois assembly, as a young lawyer in his famous debates with Stephen Douglas, and as President of the United States, Abe's skill as a speaker won him respect and admiration.

Abe worked as a postmaster, a surveyor, and a farmhand before he was elected to public office. People who knew him trusted him. The poor backwoods boy grew up loving people, the land, and the law. One day, he would prove his love for all of these by serving as his nation's sixteenth president. He would lead his country through the worst days of the Civil War and give new meaning to the word "liberty."

INDEX

Look for these other exciting
EASY BIOGRAPHIES:

Abigail Adams

Elizabeth Blackwell

Marie Curie

Amelia Earhart

Thomas Edison

Albert Einstein

Helen Keller

Martin Luther King, Jr.

Rosa Parks

Harriet Tubman

George Washington

The Wright Brothers